Win at the Game of Life

RETIRE IN YOUR 30S

The Ultimate Guide to Financial Independence

Jagoda Minorska

DISCLAIMER

This book is not intended as a substitute for professional financial advice. Everything is written based on personal experience. It is not intended for the reader to take the author's experience as a symbol of reliable information. The reader should consult a professional before making any financial decisions. This book is solely written for entertainment purposes. The ideas presented in no way guarantee financial success. The author and agents assume no responsibility for errors or omissions. Nor do they assume liability or responsibility to any person or entity with respect to any loss or damages arising from the use of information contained herein.

CONTENTS

Introduction

The journey of early retirement has changed my life. Not long ago it never even crossed my mind that this could be an option. You had to go to college, get a job and retire in your 60s at the earliest. There just wasn't another way of doing things. No one presented me with alternatives. No one even mentioned the idea of early retirement.

While in college and after graduating I was working multiple jobs at once. They were all in different fields and after a few years, I knew there had to be a different way. I could not do this forever. I always thought that I was good at saving, growing up in a family with huge financial struggles will do that to you. Because I was working so much, I was finally was able to save up enough and get my first taste of traveling. After seeing a different corner of the world, I was shocked at everything that I was missing out on. Just having two weeks a year to see the world was not going to cut it. I made it my mission to change my lifestyle, experience more and be free.

I became obsessed with gaining more income and optimizing savings. I also learned that I could be even better at saving in so many ways. I learned that I could make my money work for me and it would bring in more money. I explored endless options of passive income so that I could free up more and more time. I kept telling myself that if I don't try, I won't know, if I did nothing then nothing would change. Some of these methods succeeded and some failed. I gained so much experience and was constantly expanding my skills. Through my research, I came across the idea of early retirement. At this time the idea presented itself as retiring maybe 10 or a maximum of 15 years early. I learned all of the ins and out. This became my ultimate goal. After beginning the journey, I started to think that I could be financially free even faster. I just needed to commit and dedicate myself in the beginning to reach that goal of freedom for the rest of my life.

I know that I am not the only one who's eyes lit up when they first saw the words "early retirement". After all, some type of desire made you want to read about it too.

CHAPTER 1

Retirement is when you withdraw from your occupation, and you have sources of income that do not have to be earned by working. This is usually because you have reached retirement age. The age of retirement across the globe is between 60 to 65 years, after which there is usually a national system of pensions or other methods of benefits for retirees. But here we are talking about early retirement. So, what exactly is early retirement?

Early retirement means financial independence at a certain age when it is not precisely forced upon you. When you want to stop working before average retirement age and live the rest of your life off of your savings and investments. Moreover, it also means that you want to travel across the world without having to worry about your job, money, and work deadlines. Or maybe you have kids, and you want to spend time with them without any deadlines. Either way, it means you have saved enough money while working, and now you are ready to live your life freely without ever having to work again. You have a plan, and all you need to do is put it into action.

In short, it means to make, save, and invest money. All these things combine to help you achieve your goal. But what is your goal? Can a person retire as early as in their 30s? I say, of course, they can! But this is a long journey that not many people want to complete. It demands a proper money mindset along with an appropriate plan for money-saving to set you up with the kind of lifestyle you want during your retirement. Retiring in your 30s is quite daunting because it is a challenging journey. It usually takes about 10 to 16 years, depending on your situation. You typically have to save up until your savings are at least 40% or hopefully more of your annual income. It may vary for each individual. This usually means making sacrifices now in order to reach freedom later. I have also covered this topic in detail. So, if you are thinking about or planning to retire early and in your 30s, keep reading because I have some great tips and plans lined up for you throughout this book. I am more than sure that if you read this through, you will be able to get your answers and you will find your goal achievable as well.

My only rule for you is to mark your calendar and reread this book in 30 days. Reflect on what you have done in those 30 days. Realign as to whether you are on the right track. Do this every 30 days until you are financially free.

Start with A Proper Money Mindset

When you want to retire in your 30s, the first and the most significant step in your journey is to have a proper money mindset. Shift your mindset from scarcity to abundance. With a scarcity mindset, you'll find yourself always focusing on never having enough. As you may have guessed, an abundance mindset is the exact opposite. An abundance mindset keeps in mind every possible favorable outcome for your financial situation while allowing you to be open to each one.

We all have feelings that we associate with money, for a lot of people this may be fear, guilt or jealously. For example, if you see someone driving down the street in your favorite sports car and you think "I'll never be able to afford that" you have a negative money mindset. This has a disastrous effect on your financial situation because what you think affects how you feel and the actions that you take.

Since childhood, everyone has created limiting beliefs about money that we have accepted to be true. The idea that money can't buy happiness and that you can't be rich and a good person.

You cannot build a positive money mindset if you have any negative feelings towards money. You need to identify and address any of these limiting beliefs. Start to love money. Money is not the root of all evil and being wealthy is a good thing! Money is accessible and allows you to do what you want when you want.

To change this mindset, you can use positive affirmations. Tell yourself "I am creating all of the money I could ever want. I can accomplish anything I want to do in life". Repeat "Money is coming to me in expected and unexpected ways". Know that "I am a money magnet".

Visualize your wealth as if you've already achieved it. Visualizing a world where you have all the money you desire not only creates a mindset that is more receptive to financial gain, it also enables you to imagine what your life would be like once you reach your goals. See the money that you don't have as something abundant and acquirable, while at the same time see the money you do have as a tool that can be used to make more money rather than something that has to be protected because you are scared to lose it.

As you start to adopt a positive money mindset don't forget about the power of gratitude. Truly being grateful for something tends to eliminate any limiting beliefs. Be thankful for the money that you have, the opportunities that it has given you and the opportunity to make more money. No matter how much or how little money you are earning right now, your mindset will dictate how much you will earn in the future. Focus on attracting what you want.

The other way that your mindset will have to change is more focused on habits, specifically money spending habits. This usually means adopting a more frugal lifestyle. Personal savings orientation means that you have a more goal-oriented and motivated lifestyle and routine. Having a money-saving lifestyle isn't just something you achieve overnight. Your current habits won't change automatically. You will need to be motivational and optimize any opportunity of money-saving that you stumble upon to enhance your saving experience. The best example is that of a rubber band. Too much too early and too fast won't help you at all, and you will end up achieving nothing. Small and baby steps would instill the habits into you and do the job in the long-run. When you first think of saving, you can start with the bare minimum. Set up small goals for yourself and then move onto big things. Having a frugal lifestyle would require a financial budget, which is why I have given you some great tips to make one and also a template that you can follow.

This is building a foundation on which your dreams will stand. Having a proper money mindset will help you see the whole picture more clearly. This includes making a budget for financial independence, reaching or applying that budget into your lifestyle and starting to save as early as possible.

What is a Financial Independence Budget?

The very first step on this journey is to make a budget, and for financial independence, you will make a financial independence budget. Why is it called this? Because this budget is entirely different from any other budget. The sole focus of this budget is to achieve your freedom. Many people don't like to make budgets. When the word budget comes up you will hear them complaining that it is too much of a hassle, and their mind can't take all the counting and calculating. So, if you are one of these people, make sure you get over the fear because having a budget is a must, and without it, you simply cannot achieve your goal.

You cannot dive head forward into retirement without knowing where your money is going, and this budget will help you see step by step how you should spend your money. Also, this budget will make sure you are utilizing all available options and optimizing every single chance. How will you start? When you make your budget, you have to make sure you are as accurate as you can be. Your history in terms of spending habits and the amount of money coming in will help.

You will start with income. This includes income from your full-time job, if you have any rental property's or any side/free-lancing work too. Whatever side hustles you do will increase your income flow. You can add in whatever sources you are earning from. If you don't have any side hustles right now, don't worry, I will give you plenty of ideas. This part is essential because diversity in your sources of income is like laying a solid and sturdy foundation for your goal of financial independence. One of the main focuses in our financial independence budget is making more and saving more. Although studies show that earning more is not directly proportional to saving more. This is why knowing your spending habits and optimizing them is so important.

Once you know exactly how much money is coming in, the first expense is always going to be yourself. Pay yourself before starting to pay others. What is paying yourself? This is the amount that you keep aside for your future. Before you buy anything or pay any bills set aside a portion of your income to save. The first bill you pay each month should be to yourself. This is probably the exact opposite of what you are doing right now, and most people consider this at the very end of their budget.

Paying yourself first also allows you to build an emergency fund. Your emergency fund will be enough money for you to live off of for at least six months and ideally two years. Sometimes life is unpredictable, and you can lose your job or have a large unexpected expense. Your emergency fund will give you something that you can easily fall back on without having to liquidate investments. My tip is when you reach your six-month emergency fund goal, you still keep adding into it. This way after you retire early you can have enough money to fall back on in case the economy is not optimal. This money should be kept in a high yield savings account. A high yield savings account is not going to make you much money, but at the very least it will keep your money from depreciating due to inflation. I will talk this in detail along with discussing all kinds of other accounts in Chapter 4.

Another subsection in paying yourself is your retirement accounts like 401K or Roth IRA. These accounts need to be fully taken advantage of along with employer matches to your contributions. The main difference between these two accounts is that with a 401K you invest pretax dollars, lowering your taxable income for that year. With a Roth IRA, you invest after-tax dollars, which means your investment will grow fax-free. My recommendation is to invest in your 401K up to the matching limit, then fund a Roth up to contribution limit. The money in these accounts can be withdrawn without penalty once you are at the age of 59 ½. But we are not waiting that long to retire so stocks and bonds are going to be very important to us. Stocks and bonds will make your portfolio grow and if done right this is definitely something that you can live off of for the long run.

Next, you should focus on living expenses like rent, mortgage, internet, bills, maintenance, insurance, and cell phones. You can alter this according to your lifestyle. In chapter 2 I even have a few hacks the let you live rent and mortgage.

Then comes the food section, this includes groceries, eating, coffee, and drinks. This section does depend upon your needs, but for financial independence or early retirement, you must know what your needs and wants are. Food usually costs people a lot, so this section is going to deserves a lot of attention from you. Everyone can bring their food budget down and in chapter 2 I show you how along with why.

The transportation budget all depends on you how much you want to spend on it. You can make this budget as small as possible if you want to. Remember walking or biking is always an option and you can have a simple reliable car instead of a fancy brand new one. I have also covered all this in chapter 2. Transportation can include car insurance, public transportation, maintenance, fuel, and vehicle registration.

Next comes personal care, this includes clothes for kids and adults, haircuts, school and art supplies, gym membership, etc. Again, this section can cost a lot more than needed when you don't know how to make a budget and you give into consumerism. To achieve financial independence at an early age, most people need to restructure their personal care spending. Personal care is a must, but you don't need to spend a lot on it. Just like you don't need a new outfit for every event.

When it comes to travel, I want your airfare budget to be zero. This does not mean that you can't fly. The reason is that one of the great ways of achieving financial independence and still travel is by travel hacking. I will show you exactly how to do this later. This section can also include any hotels/Airbnbs, rental cars, travel insurance, etc.

I am talking about debt last but don't let this fool you, paying off your high-interest debts is a priority. It is very reasonable to not invest much and instead focus more on paying off your high-interest debts at the beginning of your journey. This can be credit cards, student loans and any other debts of yours. I am not adding mortgage here because I have covered it in the household category, and it is usually not a high-interest debt.

Now you have created yourself a budget template that will give you an exact outline of how much money is coming in and how much is leaving. You may be shocked at the cost of some sections and you can highlight those for change.

You should calculate your savings percentage, both monthly and annually. If you are saving even 30% to 40%, then you are doing good, and 50% means you are ahead of the game. The savings rate in this world and especially in the U.S. is meager. This budget also lets you track your expenses, and you can see where you are spending more or less so that you can alter respectively in that area. This budget is an excellent tool in your journey of retiring early and financial independence. You can use it however it suits you. In short, it lets you evaluate your current lifestyle and tracks your spending.

I have created an example of a possible budget for a single person that way you can get an idea as to how to organize your own. I am not saying this is a good or bad breakdown, everyone's situation is completely different, feel free to add or subtract categories. Your own budget should also change over time as your needs change. Once you see how much you are sending in each category decide how much you actually need to spend there. Most people send around $500 a month on unnecessary expenses. If you can even save a few hundred dollars it will make all the difference in the long run. Each month reevaluate, make sure you are still on track and see if you can minimize even more.

Income	Annual	Monthly
Full time job	$48,000	$4,000
Passive income	$3,000	$300
Property rent	$10,800	$900
Side jobs	$2,000	$200
Total	$63,800	$5,400
Expenses		
Pay yourself	$41,500	$3,365
401(k)	$19,500	$1,625
IRA	$6,000	$500
Emergency fund	$1,200	$100
Brokerage	$14,800	$1,233
Living		
Rent	$7,200	$600
Gas bill	$1,200	$100
Phone bill	$600	$50
Insurance	$600	$50
Cable/Internet	$720	$60
Maintenance	$840	$70
Food		
Groceries	$2,400	$200
Restaurants	$1,200	$100
Coffee	$360	$30
Drinks	$360	$30
Transportation		
Gas	$2,400	$200
Car insurance	$1,200	$100
Tolls	$60	$5
Registration	$40	$40
Personal Care		
Clothing	$600	$50
Gym	$240	$20

membership		
Salon	$180	$30
Travel		
Airfare	$0	$0
Hotel/Airbnb	$600	$200
Debt		
Student loan	$1,200	$100

PERSONAL BUDGET

Total Monthly Expenses = $2,035
Total Yearly Expenses = $22,300

Total Monthly Savings = $3,365
Total Yearly Savings = $41,500
Savings rate around 65%

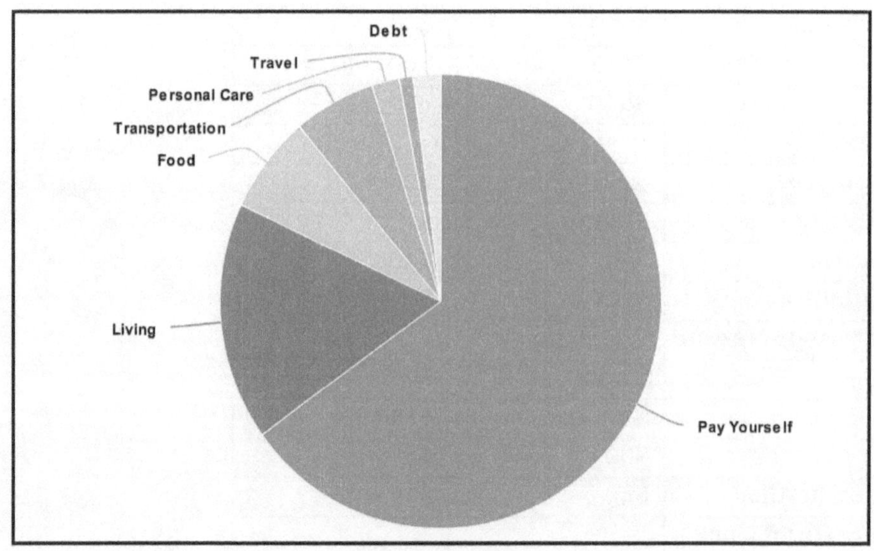

Tips to Save More

I believe that people can save 65% to 70% of their income if they really want to. Half of the battle during this journey of early retirement is to save more and start saving as early as possible. I have covered how you can save on specific things in chapter 2. But here are some tactics to help you with smart saving.

Buy Nothing Group

You can join a buy nothing group. It sounds crazy, doesn't it? And you probably have never heard of them. Buy nothing groups are a movement that has been going on for a long time. There is a website, buynothingproject.org that will help you. When you visit the site, you can find your local buy nothing Facebook group. You will find people there with similar interests, they share some fantastic tips and recycling tactics to help each other on their journey. The group allows people to gift each other items that they no longer want for free. The idea is to post anything that you want to give away, lend or share with neighbors. The free section of Craigslist and Freecycle can have some hidden gems too. Usually, the people who post there are moving and just don't have the time to sell items. They need it gone as fast as possible so act quick!

Familiarize Yourself with Sharing

Another idea is to join a social media page or website where you can share items and get ideas for free. You can also form these kinds of groups with your family and friends so that you can share the items that you don't need and in return get something that you want, for free. One example of that is baby clothes. When your friend's daughter outgrows her clothes, your friend can share the clothes with you to help you save money. Then when your friend has another daughter you can give the clothes back to her. The main concept here is to be open to the idea of sharing, and you can go pretty long without buying much when you create a big enough community.

72-Hour Rule

A great rule for saving money is the 72-hour rule. When you want to buy certain items, make a list of these items. Then after 72 hours, come back to that list and determine which things you want and if you're going to buy them or not. This rule saves you from impulse buying because, after this much time, you will be able to decide on what you need and what you might have just wanted at the moment. This tip works pretty well with children as well. Whenever you go to a store, and your child wants to buy something, give them 72 hours, and after this much time, either he/she will be less likely to want it or will forget about it.

Go for Generic Items When Shopping

Generic brand items are usually significantly cheaper than name-brand items. Using generic brand items in your meals will save you a few dollars per meal. I find that some of the biggest savings here can also be in household cleaning supplies. Remember the generic brand is the same thing as the name brand item just in different packaging. But also remember to still read prices and pay attention because I have defiantly come across times where the generic brand is a little more expensive or in smaller packaging for the same price.

Pay Yourself First

I touched on paying yourself first earlier, but this is just so important. Usually, people spend money on the "necessities" first, and whatever remains at the end goes to themselves. By paying yourself first, that amount goes directly into your savings, and it is one of the greatest ways to save more. It's like the money isn't even there and it is not an option to spend it. Every single time you pay yourself first, you will save more than when you paid yourself last. After pinching pennies and paying everything else remember to give yourself a bonus any leftover money.

Evaluate your Expenses

You can always save more by evaluating your expenses. Go deep into every cost and assess it. This can be overwhelming but do it one section at a time. For example, you take your life insurance plan, evaluate it, analyze it, and see if there are other plans which are more feasible, and then you move onto your next category. Remember to shop around once a year when it comes to insurance, rates are always changing.

Create a Budget

You already know how to do this! Once you know how much you are spending in each category and you have evaluated your expenses you can create a budget. This means tracking all of your expenses and spending. You want to know where every penny is going that way you are not overspending in any category.

Find Free Entertainment Options

There are always free things to do in every area. You can get books for free, movies, fitness classes, the list is enormous. Join your local library and look at Facebook events. For example, near me just this week there is free yoga at the park and a free community concert. You can also always ask for discounts and bargains too. Many places do student discounts or have deals going on that you may not know about.

Educate Yourself

The last one is to educate yourself. Read books, watch videos on YouTube, and listen to podcasts. Don't try to reinvent the wheel. It is all about getting familiar with what works for other people. There are always tips and tricks to learn. This will help you optimize your savings and you will be virtually surrounding yourself with likeminded people.

CHAPTER 2

In the previous chapter, I talked all about tracking your spending, what early retirement is and what the first steps are. You learned the skill of tracking all your income and expenses, and how to make a financial independence budget. In this chapter, I will further cover this topic of savings because we all know that the second and the most crucial step in this journey of early retirement is saving. Remember that the person who makes an income of $60,000 but saves 30% is better off than the person who makes $300,000 and spends it all. Keep reading, and you will get many questions answered.

Saving is essential for two main reasons. When you increase your rate of saving; your spending rate is lower, and this directly enables you to retire early. The second one is by saving more; you are putting more money into your investment accounts, which will grow with each passing month.

Now when I say saving is the most crucial step this still means that you have to make enough money. The focus should be how on can you make more rather than not increasing income and saving a few extra dollars here and there. When you are making more, it does not mean you can spend more. Stick to a very frugal lifestyle no matter what your income is.

When I say frugal, I don't want you to automatically think cheap. Both cheap and frugal people love to save money. Being cheap is about spending less; being frugal is about prioritizing your spending so that you can have more of the things that you really care about. Frugal people asses the bigger picture and have patience, value is the bottom line. While cheapness uses the price as the bottom line and value saving money no matter the real cost. Those who are cheap think that their money has to be guarded at all times and they are afraid to spend it. They are willing to sacrifice quality, value, integrity and time for short term savings. An example of this is when a cheap person goes out to eat, they will barley leave a tip. Not leaving a tip is perfectly legal and they will pay for their food. While a frugal person will choose an appetizer instead of an entrée, get water or even just go to a quick-service restaurant that you don't tip at. A cheap person will always buy the lowest cost item.

In the long run, a cheap person will end up spending more money replacing these things over and over again. While the frugal person waited for the high-quality item to go on sale and it will last them forever. Yes, this is a fine line but the side that you step on makes all the difference.

I am going to give you so many tips and tricks to save money and be frugal. One of everyone's biggest expenses is housing or accommodation. I have some great tips and tricks for you to purchase a home in a costly market. You can save hundreds and thousands if you apply these ideas.

Live Large

Did you know anyone can live rent-free and mortgage-free in a house? Sounds impossible, right? I am so excited to unveil the secret as to how you can also do this. Housing is one of our most significant expenses, and a recent study at Harvard has proved that around 35 million people in America are unable to afford their own homes.

If you are a student, you can become an apartment manager or resident advisor (RA). But this advantage is only for students. So, if you are not a student, then you can become an in-house apartment manager, which is the alternative of resident advisor. In-house apartment managers have the same role and responsibilities as an RA.

House Hacking

Another way that you can live rent-free even in the most expensive city or neighborhood is by house hacking. House Hacking is a strategy that involves renting out portions of your primary residence to generate income. This income is used to offset the cost of your mortgage and other expenses associated with owning a home. When done correctly, it allows people to live in expensive areas completely for free, or even generate positive income through homeownership. Not too shabby right? House hacking can save you money by lowering your taxable income base. You will acquire extra tax write-offs. You will benefit from owner-occupant financing which has lower interest rates and more attractive terms than investment financing. If you keep the property as a long-term rental, this is a huge benefit because you can keep the owner-occupied loan in place even after moving out. Smaller down payments of 0% to 5% are possible with programs like VA and FHA loans. Typical investment loans require 20-25% down. You will also gain experience in being a landlord and transition into the world of real estate investing.

Start with a multi-family home, the more units the better. You will live in one unit and rent out the others. The income that you generate from the rental units will pay your mortgage and you will have no out of pocket payment. In many cases, you will be able to pay the mortgage every month and have extra rental income too. Letting you not only live for free but also make an extra profit. Do put some of this profit aside in case any house repairs come up.

Rent it

Another option is renting out extra rooms. This can be in your home, a finished basement or maybe if you have additional dwelling units (ADU's). ADU's are self-contained housing units on the ground of a single-family home. It can be attached or detached from the main home. ADU's are great to rent out long term or short term on Airbnb and VRBO. You also don't have to be a landlord to use Airbnb and VRBO. You can have an agreement with your property owner to rent out your rooms or even your entire house. The contract should be made beforehand because some leases forbid it. Feel free to get creative and rent out a mobile home or RV. You can even rent parking spaces in your driveway on sites like pavemint.com, spothero.com, and curbflip.com.

Downsize

The other way you can live rent-free is by downsizing. If the place that you live in has extra space that you don't need than you can rent it out and get a condominium. With the money you get from renting, you will be able to pay the mortgage for your condo and have money left over. What usually happens is someone buys a big house in a great neighborhood. They do minor low-cost renovations, things that don't require hiring a contractor. Then after living in it, they realize the space is too big. Or maybe they start adopting a more frugal lifestyle and want to downsize. You can rent out the space, get a small fixer-upper and repeat the process. With the rent from the big house, you should be able to afford your mortgage on that house and your condo. This is a compelling tactic, and more and more people are adapting it to save. Downsizing is very helpful, and you can live large in a small house. This means less housing costs and more savings.

This also overlaps with the BURRRR strategy. BURRRR stands for buy, rehab, rent, refinance, repeat. The idea is to get a great deal on a rental property that you can add value to through making repairs. Once you buy the property you need to fix it up so you can easily rent it at a higher rate start making money. By refinancing it you can take most or all of your money back out to invest in more properties. Once you get your money back, you can find another great deal to buy and repeat the process. An example of this is if you buy a house for $100,000 that needs $15,000 in repairs. The house will be worth $155,000 once those repairs are done. When you refinance the house, you can get a loan for $116,250. The new loan will pay off the first loan you got when buying the house, plus it covers all the repairs.

Real Estate Hacks

When looking to buy real-estate one of the first things you can do is to look up your city's master plan. While house hunting, always refer back to the master planner. It will provide you with a layout showing the projected developmental areas in your town. These plans are very easy to read because they are written for the public. A master planner would essentially tell you what to expect for the future. Now you have to find a great deal before the development comes. This way your housing value will only keep increasing. Another little trick is to look during the winter or more specifically between Thanksgiving and Christmas. This is because there is low competition, so houses are the cheapest and you can take full advantage.

Search for a place where the seller is still in the home and it is not staged a home. Staged homes usually sell for so much more than the houses in which the seller hasn't tried to do anything to make it look pretty. You can ideally get that house without any competition, later you can stage it and sell it for profit.

When going to look at real-estate a great tool that you can use is <u>Redfin</u>. It lets you schedule a meeting within a few hours or sometimes, even in half an hour. It is different from a regular real estate agent where they make an appointment that suits both parties. With Redfin, you can get one according to your timetable. It will also give you a rebate when you use them. Meaning that after the home is closed, they will pay you a portion of their commission back.

Some Hacks for Free Travelling

Everyone loves to travel but no one likes the cost associated with seeing the world. Traveling usually means using a big chunk of your savings. But what if I told you there are ways to travel for absolutely free? Yes, there are ways. Because studies suggest that around 70% of Americans go into debt when they go on vacation. Here are some tips which will benefit you a great deal.

Travel Hacking

Travel hacking is gaining enough travel points, and award points using credit cards that it completely covers your travel costs. Start by signing up for one credit card that offers bonus miles or points. For example, the Chase Sapphire Reserve currently offers 3x points on travel and dining purchases along with a $300 annual travel credit reimbursement – just for having the card. The sign-up bonus is 50,000 miles when you charge $4,000 in the first three months. There is a $550 annual fee – but this is easily offset even by utilizing only some of the rewards. When using this method remember always to pay off your credit card in full and carry no credit card debt. To reach that spending amount, you can put your normal bills on the card. Don't spend more than you usually would just to reach the bonus. Another very basic way to avoid stress with minimum spending is to just time your reward card applications with a big purchase you need to make. For example, planning on buying a new computer? Snag a rewards card before that purchase so it goes towards the minimum spend. Did you know that you can pay your taxes on a credit card? What about your student loans? Remember it says to charge $4,000 in the first month not spend. So, turn those pesky expenses into free trips.

Make sure to check your credit score, anything beyond 650 is good enough for travel hacking. Your credit card provider often provides you with an annual report, and then there are websites like <u>Credit Karma</u> that give you a free report.

It is also good to know your traveling goals. Most specifically it is good to know which hotels you like to stay at and which airlines you love. This way you can sign up for their reward programs and gain frequent flyer miles. Over time you'll end up with many frequent flyer and hotel rewards accounts. Loyalty programs were created for this specific reason, and it works. Find the companies you like and stick with them. It's not always possible due to cost or availability but try your best to be a repeat customer. Over time these points add up to earn you free travel and hotels. To track them all, join <u>Award Wallet</u>, which is a service that helps you manage personal loyalty program accounts. To go a step further, you can always check the hotel or airline's website before you book and see if they are running any promotions that can earn you bonus miles/points.

Airlines also have their own credit cards that will give you some useful rewards. Signup bonuses are variable like for example, the Delta credit card currently gives you 70,000 bonus points when you sign up and charge $3,000 in the first three months. These 70,000 Delta points will provide you with a roundtrip ticket from America to Europe. Check what bonuses are currently offered as they are always changing.

The last tip is to rinse and repeat. Always keep an eye out for what is currently being offered and enjoy travel hacking again. Some of these tips are a little unconventional, but they work. Because any money you would normally use for your traveling is now going into your investment or savings account.

Eat Like a King

There are so many ways to save money on food. Everyone knows that avoiding eating out is number one, so I am going to start by telling you to brown bag it. Packing your own lunch will not only let you control the ingredients, so that you have a healthier meal, but it will also save you so much money. I am not buying it if you are thinking that you don't have time to make lunch. Meal prep can be your best friend. You can easily make a whole week's worth of food in under two hours while still enjoying Sunday night TV. You can even freeze single portion sizes to make your own freezer-ready meals.

Planning ahead is one of my favorite hacks. Take inventory of what you already have in your fridge and pantry. I mean look at everything. We all have items that are hidden in the back, we keep meaning to use them but always forget to. Before those items expire plan recipes around them. Make a list for any additional ingredients that you may need to pick up and make it a meal. Check ads and coupons to see if you can buy the additional items for even cheaper.

Eating healthy will not only help you feel better, but it will also save you money. Prepackaged convenience foods can really add up. You can also consider the nutritional value of food for the price. For example, flavored drinks deliver mostly empty calories, you can replace this with water and a splash of juice or a squeeze of lemon.

Look at the cost per serving and not cost per package. Instinctively if you are trying to save money you will likely reach for the least expensive bag of rice. This bag may cost you $4 and has 1 pound of rice in it, so it is $4 per pound. But if you buy the bigger bag it costs $9 and has 3 pounds of rice in it. This means the bigger bag really costs you $3 per pound. A dollar may not sound like anything to be excited about, but it can easily add up and save you a few hundred dollars a year. This is why shopping in bulk is amazing. If you have a Costco, Sam's Club or any other membership-based wholesale warehouses around you sign up. The cost of the membership will pay for itself in the first few trips. This is not only great for families either. An individual person might not be able to finish two loaves of bread before they go bad, or a whole tray of cookies, but don't be afraid to freeze things. Bread, vegetables, fruit, meats, deli slices, cheese, and whole sandwiches can even be frozen.

This also transitions into shopping seasonally. Not only does food taste better when it is in season, but it is also cheaper. Stock up and enjoy your favorites at a low cost all year long. Buying strawberries during the summer and freezing them for smoothies in the winter is an amazing way to not have to go out and buy those overpriced flavorless winter berries. Take advantage of prices when you can. Roasts are on sale during the holidays. You can throw them whole into your freezer. Around the 4th of July hotdogs, condiments and chips are always on sale. Stop throwing away those grocery store flyers and actually look at them.

When possible substitute meats for inexpensive vegetarian protein sources. You can even eat vegetarian a few times a week to not only increase your consumption of healthy plant foods but also to help the environment and save money at the same time. You can also minimize your portions of meat and extend the dish with more whole grains, beans or vegetables.

Always repurpose food. The Environmental Protection Agency estimates that Americans throw away about 30 million tons of food each year. So, let's say you had a party and have a whole sandwich platter left over. No one wants to eat the same thing over and over again, but no one wants to waste food either. You can repurpose those sandwiches and make a cheesy sandwich bake. Make croutons or breadcrumbs out of the bread and chop up the meat and cheese for omelets. Or you can just stick them in the freezer and have an on the go lunch whenever you need it. This method can be used for meal prep too. You can make a big batch of rice for the week and use it in tacos, on salads, as a side, mix in some sauce or make fried rice.

Money-Saving Plan and Retirement Period

It is commonly assumed that early retirement is a long process, and you cannot achieve it in less than 20 to 30 years. But let me tell you that if you have a proper money saving plan, a retirement plan and you know how to save more, make more and decrease your expenses, then you can retire early and in about 10 to 12 years.

Your savings rate can be measured by calculating how much you earn and subtracting how much you spend. For example, if you make $250 and spend $250, then your savings rate is 0%. But if you make $250 and spend $125, then your savings rate is 50%. There are a few ways to increase your savings rate. You can lower your expenses, or you can earn more and keep your expenses the same or ideally you can earn more and lower your expenses.

Here I will focus on reducing your expenses. Early retires set aside as much money as possible to live a financially free life. But a good question to ask is, once you have all the savings you want, what do you do with it? The answer is you invest it. When you invest your money is working for you and it grows with compound interest. There will come a time where it will grow enough to support your retirement. And that's how you retire early and live off your investments. Studies suggest setting a goal of having a portfolio that is worth 25 times more than your annual spending, this is because of the 4% rule. According to retirement research, an individual would never run out of money if they withdraw just 4% of their investments every year once they have reached the amount calculated above. This is because the average market rate of return is higher than 4%. In other words, when you are making a minimum of 4% interest from your investments every year, you are living off of that interest every year, and you don't have to touch the principle. For example, an average American household makes about $60,000. 30% goes into housings, 20% to 25% into the food, 10% to 15% in clothing, 15% to 20% in transportation, 12% to 15% in medical, 3% to 5% on entertainment. Their savings rate is 10% to 15% at maximum. And they can retire in about 50 years. But then there is a family pursuing early retirement. They make just the same $60,000, but their housing costs are 0% by House hacking, which is discussed above in this chapter. Food is 10% to 15% because they don't eat out, shop from sales, buy in bulk, pre-plan their meals and create grocery lists, a total decrease of 50%. Clothing is 3% to 7% due to having minimal wardrobes and shopping second hand when needed. Transportation is 5% to 7% because either they prefer to walk or get used cars, which results in the low price of their vehicle, fewer sales tax, less insurance premium, and fewer interest payments as well. Medical and Entertainment is the same, but the total savings rate has increased to 60% - 67%, which enables them to retire in 10 to 12 years. So, the math is simple, and the techniques are tricky, but I have you covered.

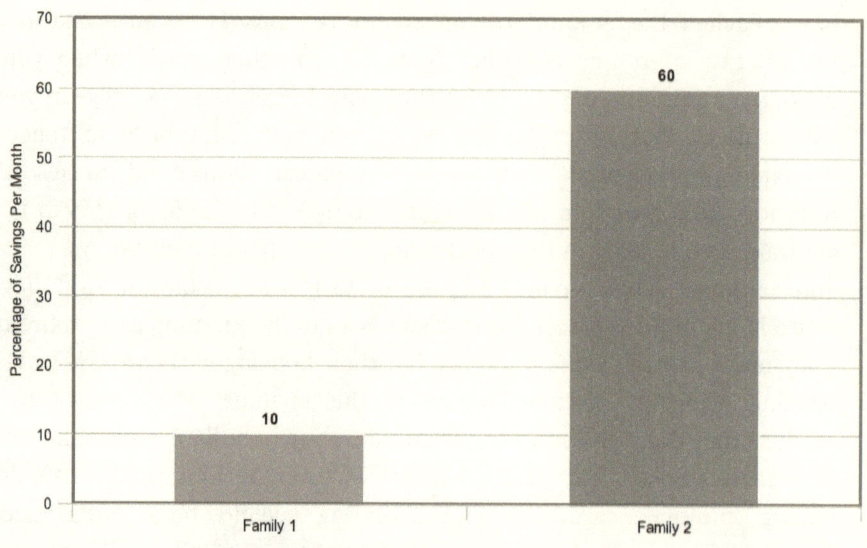

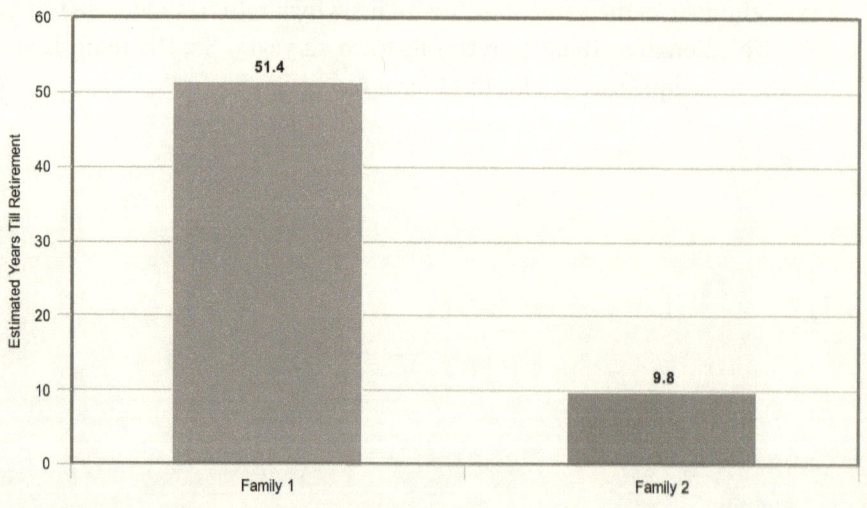

Can you save money but still get the things you want?

During the journey of early retirement, it is imperative that you save as much money as you can. Fortunately, there are many wants that don't require spending at all, but people don't usually know that. So, here are some amazing tips that will get you what you want for free so that you can focus on saving.

My first tip is for eating out and especially if you have kids. Your kids can eat out for free at so many places. There is a website mykidseatfree.com, and it probably has 5000 restaurants that let kids eat for free. You put in your state and city, and it gives you all the restaurants. An example is IKEA, they have this arrangement every Wednesday.

Now, if you pay a lot for printing your photos, then you can download an app called Shutterfly. The app has this amazing feature where you get unlimited 4x4 and 4x6 printed photos. There is also unlimited photo storage through the app that way you can access your photos from any device.

This one is for those people who love sprucing up photos in Photoshop. Now, we all know Photoshop is a costly software. So, you can use GIMP, which is a free alternative to Photoshop. GIMP can be used for image retouching and editing, free-form drawing, converting between different image formats, and more specialized tasks.

This next tip is for long drives. There is a website called autodriveaway.com, that transports vehicles from one state to another state. You can sign up as a driver and get paid to deliver these vehicles. Find a vehicle that needs to be delivered to the area that you would like to go and don't spend money on gas or a rental.

As far as reading we all know that you can go to a library and check out books for free. But there is also a website gutenberg.com that has 50,000 eBooks available for free. Many of these books have expired copyrights so you can download them for free. The website does look a little like its stuck in the early 90s but if you can get past that there are so many great books to choose from.

If you need to do repairs on your car but don't have the right tools you can borrow them from auto part dealers. Some places like <u>Pep Boys</u> and <u>Auto Zone</u> allow you to pay a deposit, use their tools, return them, and get your full deposit back. You can also borrow a large variety of tools from your local tool lending library as well. Use <u>Local Tools</u> to see if there is a lending library near you and get tools completely free.

There are also ways to get free services for your car at Auto Parts Retailers. <u>Pep Boys</u> and <u>Auto Zone</u> will do tests on your brakes, alignment, battery, alternator, and starter. They can even charge your battery, do code retrieval and install windshield wipers all for free.

When it comes to internet you can use <u>WiFi Map</u>. It will help you locate all the free internet zones in your neighborhood. The internet can be from different restaurants, cafes or just community WIFI spots.

Learning a foreign language can open so many new doors for anyone but it doesn't have to cost as much as a trip to a foreign country. There are many foreign language classes available on the internet, and they are expensive, but <u>Duolingo</u> offers its courses for free on their website and their app. They teach vocabulary, phrases, sentence structure, and conjugations. The lessons are bite-sized so you can get one done when you are just trying to kill a few minutes. Duolingo really makes it fun by allowing you to earn points for correct answers, race against the clock and level up.

For movies Netflix, is pretty cheap, but if you don't want to spend a single penny, then there are many services that you can still use. <u>Sony Crackle</u> allows you to stream free movies and shows. The choices are a little older, but they do offer great classics and unique films.

CHAPTER 3

You can only save so much; the real goal is to make more to be able to save more. Always focus on increasing your income. This means at your full-time job, your passive income and engaging in side-hustles so that you can make the most out of your time and reach your goals quicker.

Prioritize your career. Before you take on any additional work make sure that your career will still come first. Don't stay up all night working a side job, come into work tired every morning and expect to succeed. Grow your skills, impress your boss and build a strong professional network. Become the best in your field so that you can get that raise or land a higher paying job at a different company.

Ideas for passive income

Passive income is income that requires little to no effort to earn or maintain. It is also progressive passive income when the earner expands little effort to grow the income. Passive income means that you have bundled up your labor in such a way that you don't have to labor every day, but it still gives you profit.

Patreon

The first idea I have for you is Patreon.com. This is a website that allows patrons to support creators. The idea is that people give donations to support creators on their work. Now, creators can be writers, YouTubers, musicians, podcasters, or any kind of bloggers. Patrons is set up as a monthly subscription. Your supporters can pay $1 a month as a necessary payment. They can also give you $5 a month so that they can have early access to specific content. $10 a month means they want some extra content or videos from you. It even goes to $20 or much more for getting behind the scenes content from the creator. It is a great way to earn money for those who are already making content. It allows people to support creators so that they can continue their work. The fantastic thing about Patreon.com is that the creator is in full control of their content and can retain 90% of the money received.

Etsy

I'm sure most people have heard of Etsy, a great marketplace for homemade soaps, handknit scarves and much more. This website is essentially a marketplace for creators. But here I am talking specifically about digital downloads. This means that you create something just once. For example, a bookmark, a calendar, or a notebook design, you put it on Etsy, and people purchase the download. When you search digital download products on Etsy, you stumble upon a wide variety of ideas. They include cards, templates, patterns, photography prints, and lots of other things. You create it once, and it continues to earn you money. How will you create your designs in the first place? You can use Canva.com. It is a fantastic free design app and a website that even has templates for flyers, brochures, invitations, wallpapers and so much more. You can also use Gimp, which as mentioned earlier is a free alternative of Photoshop.

Amazon Affiliate Links

Amazon does not stop growing and you can be a part of its success. One of many ways to enjoy the benefits is to take advantage of Amazon affiliate links. Amazon affiliate links work by Amazon giving you a personalized link to products. You can put your link in any social media platforms or articles that you write. When people click that link and purchase the product, you receive a certain percentage of sales. Let's say they open it but don't purchase it right away, if they purchase the product before the session expires, you will still receive a commission from that purchase. If they put something in their cart from that link and purchase it within 90 days, you will get your share too.

Online Course

Online courses are the new eBooks. They create an accessible and convenient way to learn anything. This method does require a bit more work in the beginning, but once you publish it, there is very little work other than marketing. The more you market the more money you can generate. There is a website called <u>Udemy.com</u>, where thousands of courses are available on business, makeup, writing, cooking, IT, music, graphic design, marketing, languages and so much more. The great thing about this website is that there are 24 million students who use this platform, so you would already have a huge audience who can be interested in your course.

Dividend Stocks

Dividends are paid out by company's that make so much money that they pay you for owning shares. The process of making money through dividend investing involves searching for companies that have a good chance of increasing their dividend payments year after year. When the company's sales and profits grow, so does the dividend. These stocks are also known as blue-chip stocks. A blue-chip is the stock of a well-established and historically secure corporation. They have a reputation for quality and can operate successfully in good and bad times. Think of big brands like Disney, IBM, and Coca-Cola. The biggest misconception of dividend stocks is that high yield is always a good thing. If a company is paying too high a percentage of its profits, it may be a sign that the company has little room to grow by reinvesting in its business. Aiming for a yield of 4-6% works best for most. But always do your research and look at the dividend yield in conjunction with total return as top factors. Investing in funds is also a great strategy. That way instead of putting a lot of money in one company you have a little portion of a lot of different companies that have a great reputation. An example of this is VTSAX (Vanguard Total Stock Market Index Fund) buying this mutual fund will give you exposure to the whole stock market. This is perfect for a new or passive investor because the stock market has averaged an 8.86% annual return over the past 100 years. A great strategy is known as the Three Fund Portfolio: Investing in a US stock market index, an international stock market index and a bond index. An example is about 70% in Vanguard's Total Stock Market Index – VTSAX, 20% in Vanguard's International Stock Market Index – VTIAX, and putting the 10% remaining in the Vanguard Bond Market - VBTLX. This strategy is more about investing in something completely hands-off, zero work, just set it and forget about it. To go a step further, opening a Roth IRA to hold dividend stocks lets you get the maximum tax advantage by meeting the Roth IRA contribution limit each year. An example would be investing an initial $10,000 and contributing $2,000 a month. As long as the rules of Roth IRA are followed, not a single penny is paid in taxes on the money this account makes. Investopedia has a Dividend Investment Calculator that can give you a great idea as to where your portfolio value will be over time depending on how much you want to contribute.

Kindle Publishing

With Kindle Direct Publishing you can self-publish your book and start making money in less than 24 hours. With over 90 million Prime subscribers in the United States alone, the Kindle stores reach is huge. Remember that your book cover is just as crucial as your content. It's all that Amazon will show potential buyers as they scan through lists of titles. Bright colors, bold text, and defined images help create a great cover. You can also outsource the cover design and use websites like 99designs or Crowdspring. If you want, you can outsource the whole book. Hire a ghostwriter on Fiverr or Upwork, give them a topic and publish the finished product under your name. The cost of ghostwriting can add up, but I think most people can write a short book themselves for the cost of $0 and a little time.

Have an Advertisement Placed on your Car

There is a website called wrapafy.com that will pay you up to 452$ a month to get an ad placed on your car. You download the app and they track your driving pattern for around 50 miles. Based on that they will let you know what ads you are eligible for. They call these campaigns and they last for one to twelve months. You have to be 21+ years old, your car model has to be 2008 or newer and you must have a clean driving record. You just drive around like normal and collect your check.

Buying a Property

Buying a rental property is a great way to earn a passive income. I talked about house hacking earlier and like mentioned this method will not only result in you having a free place to live, but you can also make income. Although this is not completely passive right away you can make it be. You will likely have to fix a leaky faucet or a broken dishwasher every once in a while. Yet this does not always mean you will have to do the work yourself. Knowing the right contractor or handyman to call will help. Or if you want an even more hands-off approach you can hire a property manager that will take care of everything for you.

Airbnb Your House

If you don't have an extra property or even rooms for rent, you can still take advantage of <u>Airbnb</u>. Renting out your house on Airbnb while you're traveling is a great hack. That way, you will be able to cut down on traveling expenses and make a little extra money while you are away.

Game or Website

Creating a game, or any kind of app requires skill. Most people need to put in a lot of effort, time, and hard work in the beginning. Once you put it out into the market, it would serve as a great source of passive income. There are always updates that need to be made but these can easily be outsourced. This is not an option for most people, but I had to add it in for those tech-savvy creative minds.

Affiliate Marketing

Online affiliate marketing is a revenue-sharing agreement between an online merchant and a website owner, where the website owner places advertisements on their website to send potential buyers to the merchant's website. This is usually done in one of three ways. These are pay per click, pay per lead, and pay per sale or price per transaction. If you already have a website don't forget to add advertisements. Every time people use the link, it will generate cash for you.

Influencing

When you have an audience that trusts your option affiliate marketing becomes a lot easier. With the advantage of having a following, you can also make money by doing sponsored social media or blog posts. Selling your own physical product through your platform can be a great way to kickstart a business too. It is also very popular to create an eBook or audio program to sell to your audience. You create this product once and it can generate you profit for a very long time. Video blogging can be yet another option. Being a YouTuber can definitely generate you a lot of cash, but this does require consistent dedication especially in the beginning when you won't be generating much money. Once you have a good number of videos under your belt those videos keep generating views just by being online. Influencers creating online courses has become very popular recently too.

Side Hustles

In the journey of early retirement, side hustles can make all the difference. You can work side jobs before reaching financial independence and after reaching financial freedom as well. They supplement the growth of your income no matter what stage you are at. If you don't know where to start, I have some tips and ideas for you.

Amazon FBA

Another way that you can use Amazon is through Amazon FBA, which stands for Fulfilled by Amazon. The way this works is you find a product, and you ship that product directly to Amazon. They will hold the inventory and ship the product to the customer. All you have to do is find the correct product, create the listing and maybe do a little marketing or advertising. You act as a middleman. For example, you see a product on sale at a great price, you buy all the store's inventory and put it on Amazon at a higher price. This is called retail arbitrage. You can also buy products straight from a manufacturer, it is common to use <u>Alibaba</u> or <u>Aliexpress</u>, you purchase the inventory and ship it to Amazon. When choosing suppliers on websites like Alibaba remember to always buy a sample product first and check the quality. You don't want to put your name behind something that will not get great reviews and not sell.

Delivering Packages for Amazon

Amazon is giving you get another option. There is a site called <u>flex.Amazon.com</u>, where you can pick up Amazon packages and deliver them to customers. You can make around 8$ to 25$ per hour delivering packages. They provide an app, and it calculates the way you drive. You have to use the route they give you, and they give you the quickest route so you cannot prolong your 15-minute drive and make it 30-minutes to get more money. You get to set the times and days you are available which gives you a lot of flexibility. The packages are picked up either from Amazon or other businesses.

Uber

Another driving option is <u>Uber</u>. You can decide on what hours you want to work and make money on your schedule. You must meet the minimum age requirement for your city and submit paperwork. Drivers in the US must also pass a background screening. Even if you don't have a car Uber lets you get a car from one of their vehicle partners or a fleet partner in select markets. You can also explore <u>Lyft</u> for a similar experience. If you want to take it a step-up Uber also offers Uber Fright. Or maybe you just want to drive food around instead of people, try <u>Uber Eats</u>, <u>Postmates</u> or <u>Grubhub</u>.

Reminding the Elderly

Reminding the elderly to take their medication is a side job that most people don't know about. There is a site called <u>Pleio</u> that connects caring individuals with patients. All you need is a landline or the internet and it pays around $14 to $16 per hour. The right fit is good at creating meaningful communication with patients.

Dog Sitting and Dog Walking

Dog sitting has been taken to a whole new level with technology. There is a website called Rover.com, where you can sign up to sit dogs. All you have to do is make an account, provide a little information, and you can hang out with dogs all day. With Rover, you can also set your own rate. Dog sitting is a great niche to get into because the people who have dogs really love their dogs and are willing to pay top dollar for the right care. The jobs range from overnight sitting, walks, playing with a dog and training. People usually pay you to come to their house during the day. The rates range between $10 to even $150 and up.

There is another website called wagwalking.com. It is the Uber of dog walking. When someone wants their dog to go on a walk, they open the app and pick a person close by. You pick your availability times, neighborhood's vicinity and can earn around $25 per hour plus tips. There is an application that takes about a week to get approved, and you will have to pay 25$ for the background check as well, but other than that, it is free. You can deny a walk if your busy or just don't want to do it.

Rent Out Your Car

Turo.com is a website where car owners rent out their vehicles. People usually do this if they have a new car, or if they don't use their vehicle much. It's a great way to make side money and is pretty similar to Airbnb. If you have a car that you don't use all day, you can sign up and specify the dates and times that you want to rent out your car. You set your own rate that should depend on the condition, model and year of the car. Rates usually range from $25 to $300+ a day.

Teaching English

English is an international language, and non-native speakers usually want to learn it. There are many sites where you can teach English online, but one, in particular, is SayABC. This site is great because it pays $15 to $21 for a forty-minute session. It is unique because you don't teach just one person, you can teach four people at once who all want to learn English. The only requirements of this site are that you have to be a native speaker and have a bachelor's degree. They give you all the materials you need to start teaching.

Freelancing

In terms of freelancing, you can do pretty much anything. The scope is so vast that only you can decide what you want to do. You can write, draw, record, edit, photograph, the list is endless. There are two leading websites for online freelancing which are upwork.com and fiverr.com. Earlier I mentioned hiring using these websites to outsource work, but you can be on the other side too. There is a whole world of freelancing there. The amount that you can earn here is endless.

When it comes to in-person work like landscaping, snow removal, personal training, catering, etc. you can use Thumbtack. All you have to do is create a profile, decide when, where and how you want to work, and the customers will find you. Whatever kind of work you do there is a job for you. You will be charged when an interested customer reaches out to you.

Be Your Local City Tour Guide

If you like meeting new people, chatting with them, and showing them around your city you can be a tour guide. Tourists feel like they are getting a special experience when they are with a city local. Airbnb and Showaround are the websites that you can use. You can do cooking classes, city tours, food tours and all kinds of different adventures. Pick the time and price yourself allowing this to fit around every schedule. Most simple tours can start at $25 per hour per person and go up from there. You can do some research to see what the common prices in your area are.

Tryout Software Programs

Erlibird.com pays you to test out different software programs and websites. They pay around $10 to $25 per test. You just sign up through their website, put in the devices you own, and they give you apps and other software to try. The three necessities are that; you must be 18+, fluent in English, and must own PC/Mac.

Transcribe Videos

Scribie.com is a website that needs people to transcribe audio clips. They give you 6-minute videos and you type whatever you hear. They have an automated editor, so your work isn't too hectic. You will have to fix some mistakes, but that's all. They pay around $5 to $25 per audio hour, and when you complete 3 hours, you will receive a bonus of $5. To qualify you have to pass their online test, own a computer, have a stable internet connection, and a set of headphones.

Sell your Extra Stuff and De-clutter

We all know about Craigslist and eBay but Poshmark is for high-end fashion items. Poshmark allows you to sell your handbags, jewelry, clothes, and shoes. You get to pick your prices, so it is a great way to earn money. The process involves taking a picture of your item, creating a description, and setting the price. When you make a sale, Poshmark provides you with a prepaid shipping label. They do charge a 20% fee.

Facebook Marketplace is yet another resource you can use to sell items. You take photos, add a description and name your price. You will also need to provide your location, but Facebook won't share it with anybody else, just the rough area of where you are. Facebook is not involved in the delivery or the payment, I kind of think of this as Facebook's version of Craigslist.

Another great option is to look for underpriced items. Keep an eye on all of these websites and also look at thrift stores. Particularly second-hand stores tend to sometimes not know the true value of what they are selling. There are always some great finds that you can resell for profit.

Be a Caregiver

Care.com matches caregivers with people who are looking for childcare, elderly care, household care and more. You can specify what type of service you offer, and they will connect you with the right positions. Even if your only availability is only Thursdays after 6 pm I can guarantee that you will find someone looking for a babysitter, housekeeper or personal assistant at that time. The website works across 20 countries and has 29 million users. In the U.S., they make a match every three seconds. You can choose to be a premium user for some extra perks, but it will cost you 37$ per month.

Crowdfunding

When you have an idea for an invention or have a business plan turn to crowdfunding. Maybe you don't have the amount of money you would need to start, or you want to spend elsewhere. There are websites like Kickstarter, Indiegogo, and GoFundMe, which have become very popular. These marketplaces connect people who seek funds with hundreds of investors. Your investors could be your friends or complete strangers. They just have to believe in your idea. The concept is to raise your desired amount from a large number of small contributions. You can't run off with this money as profit, crowdfunding is just a tool, but the goal is to support your idea. Getting this idea off the ground can result in a lot of profit in the long run. All you have to do is to give a small share of your profit to your investors. This depends on how you want to share these profits and what your investors want in return.

CHAPTER 4

How to Invest your Money

Through all of your income streams and your strategic saving, you should now be putting away a lot of your earning. Next, we have to talk about what can be done with those earnings to maximize your returns. You can go for investment accounts, stock market, bonds, and even savings accounts. This all depends on your situation.

Investing in the Stock Market

When you are a beginner, you may want to stay away from buying individual stocks. Investing in individual stocks properly will be very stressful for most people. It can be an emotional roller-coaster of overanalyzing and what-ifs. The game of buying and selling individual stocks is for those people that can remove their emotions and wait out the rough patches with confidence.

Low-cost index funds are a little more beginner-friendly. Index fund investing can be very profitable, and it is a lot less stressful for new players as well. I talked about the Three Fund Portfolio method in Chapter 3. This is a great hands-off approach.

Don't create an investment plan that's too complicated for you. People usually think investing is a stressful process, which it can be, but it can also be the other way around. You must keep it simple. You can start with maximizing your tax-advantaged accounts like your 401k and Roth IRA, invest in low-cost index funds, and maybe buy real estate.

You can also automate your investments to make life easier. This means putting money into the market at the same time of the month every month. You can set up automatic withdrawals weekly, bi-weekly, or monthly. The most important thing is that you consistently put money into the market. Remember to always keep learning about investments so that you can make more confident decisions in the future. It is so important to keep educating yourself.

Investment Accounts for early retirement

I have mentioned tax-advantaged accounts a few times now because everyone should be taking full advantage of these. We talked about Roth IRA and 401(k) because these are the ones that most people are familiar with. Many other types of accounts that can be right for you just depending on your goals, what kind of tax advantages you want to have and your timeline.

Below are a few options that you can consider, but you should choose those that are feasible for you and your situation. These accounts can be taxable accounts or tax-deferred accounts. The options are 401(k), Roth 401(k), 403(b), 457, Solo 401(k), SEP IRA, Simple IRA, Traditional IRA, Roth IRA, HSA (Health Saving Accounts), Brokerage accounts, 529 and Custodial accounts. These are just the main ones. You can't just choose all of them, so how do you know which ones to invest your money into?

Choose the accounts that will grow your money over the long-term even if you have early retirement goals. You must also consider the specific tax advantages that you want to implement. I am going to talk about starting with a 401(k) employer-sponsored retirement account, Roth IRA account, Traditional IRA account, HSA, custodial accounts if you have kids, brokerage account and an emergency fund (which you should already have if you are investing). Each of these accounts will play an essential role in your journey to early retirement. You're probably thinking about if there is an optimal order of investing into these accounts. Yes, there is.

When you start investing, focus on tax-deferred accounts first. The reason behind this is pretty amazing. When you invest in a tax deferring account compared to a regular account without a tax advantage, your tax-deferred account will grow so much faster than the other regular account. This is because money in a tax-sheltered or tax-deferred account is not eaten up by taxes, so it will grow more with compound interest. For example, when you invest the max 401(k) annual contribution of $19,500 into your 401(k) and add that same amount each year, your 401(k) account can grow to $392,000 in 10 years. However, that same investment into a non-retirement taxable account would grow to $322,000 if you are in a mid-tax bracket. This shows that over the period of 10 years, you will make an amazing $70,000 more because of the tax advantage. That is exactly why I have been stressing the importance of these accounts.

401(k)

Your 401(k) is essential because it will lower your taxable income and your employer can offer a 401(k) match. Your 401(k) contributions are deducted from your salary on a pre-tax basis. This means that you lower the amount you pay in current income taxes. You don't owe taxes until you withdraw your money from the plan. If your employer offers 401(k) match think of it as free money. A 401(k) match is generally set up as a percentage of an employee's salary, commonly around 6%. The employer's contribution is a certain percentage of the employee's contribution. Some employers will be generous enough to match dollar-for-dollar, or 100% contribution. Others will contribute 50% or less. Let's say you have a salary of $50,000. If you contribute 6% into your 401(k) that would be $3,000 but with a 100% match, you now have $6,000. Another good reason to take advantage of 401(k) match that this allows you to exceed the annual maximum contribution limits set by the International Revenue Service. Employer matched funds are not counted towards these limits.

Roth IRA

After you contribute to your 401(k) up to the employer match limit, you can fund a Roth IRA up to the contribution limit. A Roth IRA is funded with after-tax dollars, your money grows tax-free and you pay no taxes when you withdraw it. If your tax rate is lower now, it makes sense to pay taxes upfront in return for tax-free retirement withdrawals. You can contribute one lump sum or make smaller contributions over the course of the year, as long as your contributions don't exceed $6,000 ($7,000 if you're 50 or older). For a long-term goal like retirement, you can invest in stocks and bonds through your IRA because of their higher returns. That means opening your Roth at a brokerage or rob advisor rather than at a bank. Once you hit 59½ and have held the account for at least five years, you can take distributions, including earnings, from a Roth IRA without paying federal taxes.
You may withdraw your contributions to a Roth IRA at any time for any reason, but you'll be penalized for withdrawing any investment earnings before age 59 ½ unless it's for a qualifying reason.

Roth IRAs are a smart savings tool for young people just starting out because they're likely to face higher income tax rates as they move along in their careers. But even someone who is further along on their career path may like a Roth IRA because these accounts provide tax-free income in retirement. A traditional IRA is different: You may be eligible to take a tax deduction on your contributions in the year you put the money in, and then your withdrawals in retirement are taxed as income. If you want an immediate tax break, consider a traditional IRA. If you like the idea of tax-free income in retirement, a Roth IRA is a good idea.

HSA

Now let's talk about an HSA, which is a health savings account. If you are eligible for an HSA, then you are in for some serious advantages on your retirement journey. HSAs are triple tax-advantaged. The money that you contribute is either pre-tax, if through an employer, or tax-deductible if you open your own. You don't pay taxes on the account's growth, and you don't pay taxes on eligible withdrawals. Each year you decide how much you want to contribute to your HAS without exceeding government-mandated maximums. You can use these funds for eligible medical expenses. The great thing is that your HAS balance doesn't expire annually, which means that your money rolls over from year to year. If you don't use an HSA, then you are missing on a huge opportunity to invest your money and make it grow for you. Health costs will continue to rise, so you can use this for any emergency. There is also investment potential for HSAs. The money can be invested in mutual funds, stocks and other investment tools.

Brokerage Account

Then comes the brokerage account. I know you can put a lot of money into your brokerage account, and that's even after your tax-deferred accounts. The reason that you must invest a considerable amount of money into your brokerage account is because this account will bear your expenses in early retirement or before regular retirement age. A brokerage is a financial account that you can open with an investment firm. You can use a brokerage to purchase investments, including stocks, bonds, and mutual funds. Brokerage accounts come in all kinds of shapes and sizes. There are pricier full-service accounts and low-fee online discount brokers. Some popular and easy to use options are <u>Robinhood</u>, <u>TD Ameritrade</u> and <u>Webull</u>. You own the money in your brokerage account, and you can sell investments at any time. There is no limit to the amount of money you can deposit into a taxable brokerage account each year.

Custodial Account

Next, you could invest in your child's custodial account. We are not talking about 529 here but exclusively custodial accounts for your kids if you have any. If you don't have any kids still read through this section so that you can at least know how to make the right choices for future children or grandchildren. A custodial account is a financial account held in the name of a minor, usually by a parent or guardian. The parent or guardian will have full control of the account until the child reaches adulthood. In most cases, you will want an investment account. This gives you the ability to invest funds for the benefit of the minor. The invested income such as dividends, interest or earnings generated by the account assets is considered the child's income and taxed at the child's tax rate once the child reaches 18.

High yield savings accounts

With savings accounts, you don't usually get much interest back. Most banks typically pay you under 0.5%. The actual average is only 0.09%. A high yield savings account pays you a little better at around 2%. People don't open a savings account to get rich or wealthy. In other words, this profit is typically at the rate of inflation, which is between 1.8% and 2.2%. Inflation means the devaluation of the dollar. Every single year a dollar is worth a little less than it was last year as more money gets printed. Having money in a high-yield savings account is for short term purposes or emergency funds. It is not recommended for a long-term plan which is usually the plan during the journey of financial independence. You can put in small amounts monthly when you have some extra cash, and you can put in immense numbers as well, but when compared to investment accounts or stock funds, you will not get much return on your investment. The great thing about high-yield savings accounts altogether is that you can withdraw your money from them any time you want. These accounts are still amazing if you are putting money aside for a down payment or large purchase. That money will at least be working for you a little as save. High-yield savings accounts are also great for emergency funds. This way your money is at least not depreciating and is always there for you when needed.

How should you invest in the Stock Market?

I have talked about investing a few times now and I want to tie all of that information together because investing in the stock market is pretty amazing in the long-run.

Buy and Hold

Use the buy and hold approach when investing. This is an investment strategy practiced by passive investors who ignore the day to do and usually month to month fluctuations. The idea is to let your money increase with the growth of the overall market. Active investors attempt to make a profit from short term price movements. Yet most people can't handle market volatility. People trade emotionally, panic when the market drops or try to time the market.

Timing the market is a strategy of making buying or selling decisions by attempting to predict future price movements. The truth is no one can predict what the market is going to be doing in the short term. Time in the market beats timing the market. Let me repeat, time in the market beats timing the market. Invest immediately when you have money and keep investing. No one can predict the future so why even try.

Diversification

The number one rule is to diversify your investments. Meaning don't just invest in one sector of the stock market but in a variety of stocks, bonds and hopefully real estate. Diversification must be applied across your entire portfolio of investments. For example, you can invest all of your money into one company that you really believe in. One day the CEO could say something that the public isn't happy with or the company could create a terrible product and go under. In this case, you are putting all your cards in one basket, you will likely panic and lose them all. As discussed in previous chapters, this is why index funds are also great, you can buy the same investment over and over again to grow with the entire stock market.

Index Funds

Index funds are the best, easiest and safest investment strategy for most people. Investing in index funds requires very little work, no skill and offers you the best returns. Index funds outperform 99% of individual investors and

95% of hedge fund investors over a 10-year period. As an individual investor, those odds are definitely not in your favor. When compared to mutual funds, index funds are simple to put together and manage, meaning that those savings get passed on to you. They are known as a passively managed fund and have expense ratios of as low as 0.03%. This expense ratio automatically gets taken out so it is not something that you will even notice. Mutual funds, on the other hand, have high fees. They employ professional stock pickers who buy and sell to try to beat the market. Fees are much higher without even the guarantee of beating the market.

This idea comes back to the Three Fund Portfolio method that I mentioned in the previous chapter. To refresh your memory this is the idea that you should be invested in three unrelated markets, this way if one fails you have two others to rely on. The idea of investing in a US stock market index, international stock market index and a bond index is going to give you the broadest diversification at the cheapest cost and with the highest return overall. Index funds create stress-free stability long term. If you are looking for a very passive and hands-off approach this is for you.

Dividends

I have to circle back to dividend stocks. Investing in stocks that pay out dividends is a strategic way to establish a reliable income stream and build wealth. Dividend investing gives investors two sources of potential payout: the predictable income from regular dividend payments and capital appreciation over time. One of the most important considerations when investing is the dividend yield. Higher yields get better returns, but this can also be deceiving. You have to make sure that this payout is sustainable over the long term and doesn't run out. Sacrificing a little yield, in the beginning, can have huge payouts later. Low-risk dividend stocks may generate a lower income, but they are more reliable over time. A company's dividend payout ratio can tell you how safe an investment is. This information can tell you how much is being paid out to shareholders and how much income the company can retain. If a company is paying out a substantial percentage of its income to investors at a high yield, and the company's income stream is reduced, the number of dividends you're receiving will be greatly reduced.

The stock market moves in cycles and it has a tendency to repeat itself so there is no better prediction than a stock's past performance. Target companies that have earned "dividend aristocrat" status. These are established companies that have increased dividend payouts to investors consistently over the past 25 years. Think of the big names that everyone knows like Apple or McDonalds. This is called value investing when the company has a reliable cash flow that you can rely on. On the other side of things looking at a company's future potential is important too. This is called growth investing, when you look at the long-term potential company growth, rather than looking at what a stock is trading for currently. Spreading assets over multiple dividend-paying investments can add diversity and minimize your risk. Remember to always reinvest the dividend payments that you do receive. Dividend investing can add an exponential amount of value to an investor's portfolio.

Stick to your Guns

Understand that everyone has their own opinion. They have views on how they should invest their money and on how you should spend your money. You must stand by your research because there will be plenty of opinions, but your decision matters the most. Put your money to work. If it is sitting on the sidelines, then it is not working for you. Remember you don't really suffer a loss in the stock market unless you sell.

CHAPTER 5

When you start on your journey towards financial independence and early retirement, one of the main things to figure out is how you will live off your assets for the years to come. There must be a strategy for this, and I will give you some ideas as to how you should execute. This might look a lot different than the traditional retiree's plan. Most people retire after the age of 60, then they take their money and put it into an annuity, into CDs or cash it out. However, for an early retiree, this approach has to be a lot different. But before we begin, let me give you an investment strategy idea. Your investment strategy should be low-cost index funds and specific sectors ETFs. Then there should be investments in individual stocks, but most of your funds should be in index funds that track the stock market.

I have discussed in the previous chapter the accounts that will play a crucial role in your life when you finally retire. They should be your brokerage accounts, Roth IRA and Traditional IRA, 401k, HSA, and two years' worth of cash in a high yield savings account. Two years might sound like a lot, but when you are an early retiree, you have to prepare yourself for the unexpected. This two years' worth of money must be kept aside in the case of stock market plummets. Historically, the stock market dips last for around 14 months. You could use this money as a buffer if you don't want to draw out cash or sell your stocks but instead use your emergency fund. Using these accounts mentioned above, you are going to pay your annual expenses. I have told you how to track your costs, so this will give you an idea of how much you will need annually. Yearly payments will change once you are retired, so you would need to calculate your estimated annual expenses for retirement, and based on those numbers, you can decide on how much you will be withdrawing once you have retired.

The Famous 4% Rule

The 4% rule says that you can withdraw 4% of your portfolio value each year in retirement without incurring a substantial risk of running out of money. This rule of thumb assumes that you'll be able to generate an annual real return of 4% a year. In other words, this will let you withdraw without cutting into your investment principle.

Trinity Study

The reason I am suggesting this 4% rule is because of the Trinity study. This study was conducted by a group of finance professors at Trinity University. The study was able to calculate the retirement portfolio success rates for various monthly withdrawal rate assumptions and multiple portfolio asset allocations.

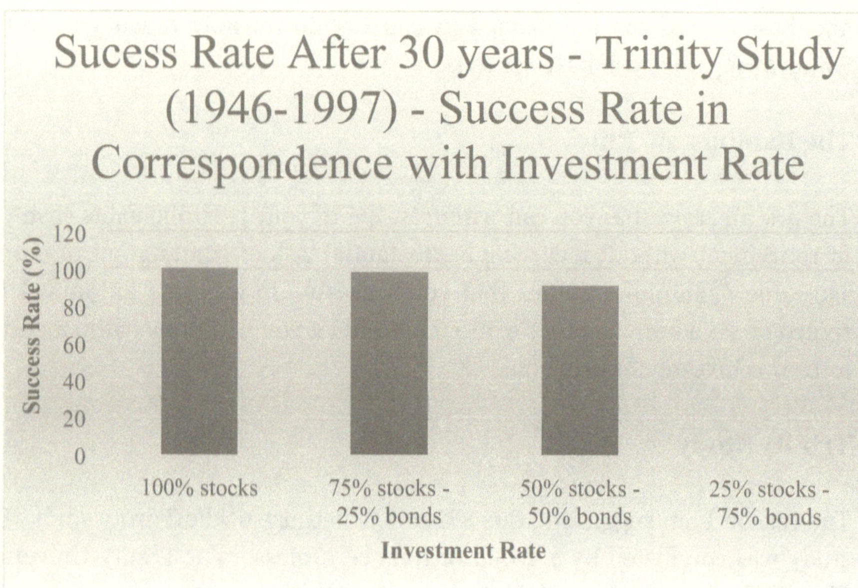

The results of the study showed that if you have a retirement portfolio that was a hundred percent stocks and you withdraw 4% from that portfolio, you would have a hundred percent success rate after 30 years. After 30 years, if you were withdrawing 4% out of a hundred percent stock investment, you would not run out of money. What is interesting is the study shows that you can do the same thing with a portfolio that consists of 75% stocks and 25% bonds, you can still have a hundred percent success rate. But, the less you have in stocks and the more in relationships, the success rate of your portfolio would start to decline, and this is counterintuitive. When most people retire, they go on the more conservative approach and move into bonds, annuities, CDs, or cash, but the Trinity study suggests that the growth would work from stock to sustain your portfolio. When it comes to bonds and CDs, their growth rate is prolonged, and they just can't keep up with inflation. The results were based on Inflation Adjusted Monthly Withdrawals from 1946 to 1997.

Another scenario shows that when you have a portfolio of 50% stock and 50% bond investment with a 4% rate of withdrawal, there would be a success rate of 91% after 30 years. But with a portfolio of 25% stock and 75% bond investment at a 4% withdrawal rate, their success would decrease to 65% after 30 years. The worst-case scenario is having a 100% investment in bonds alone with a 4% rate of withdrawal, after 30 years, the success rate would be 0% percent. This shows that you will need growth in your portfolio to sustain yourself through early retirement, and the stock market would give you the growth.

Sometimes the stock market dips, but remember, history shows us that it will rebound again and pretty much around the time frame of 14 months. When everything is going well it will give you an average return of 20% in just three years. For example, for every $100,000 that you invest in the stock market, you would get a $20,000 return.

Let's apply this 4% rule in withdrawing cash from all investment accounts. Take the cumulative of all your statements, apply the 4% rule on all of them. For example, take all of your investment accounts and calculate the sum of money that you have in them, you apply the 4% rule on the total amount of all those accounts. But you would not take 4% of all the reports. You would focus on one account and draw that amount from the one account. Since you would take from one account at a time, you could break down your drawdown strategy into two phases.

Phase one is your average at pre-retirement age (before 59), and Phase two is after retirement age. In the pure-retirement phase, you take out money from the brokerage account. You would have invested enough money in this account to know that you can live off it until you are able to use retirement accounts penalty-free. When you are withdrawing money from your brokerage account, your 401k, IRAs, and HSAs will grow at a considerable rate because of compound interest. Based on the rule of 72%, that money which you won't touch in your retirement accounts will double every nine years.

In phase one, you can also choose to live off of your dividends. This can be done along with the 4% rule or just on its own. By living off of dividends your portfolio value will not decrease while you still obtain significant income. When you are still saving, I always say to reinvest your dividends to grow your portfolio, that way your portfolio pays out even more dividends that you can reinvest. This creates a snowball effect rather quickly. Over the years as sales and profits have grown in your dividend-paying companies, so too does the dividend. The more shares you own of a high-quality dividend stock, the more money you make. Once you decide to retire early you can choose to live off of those dividends.

Now we come to the second phase. This is the retirement age phase, and you can finally access all the money from your retirement accounts. In this phase, accessing any of your accounts in any way that you want won't result in penalties. You could go for your Roth IRAs first because of the tax advantages, then HSAs, and then 401(k). Your tax situation might change, or the tax laws might change, this is why having accounts with different tax standpoints is great. Now, you must have noticed that I have been talking only about all these accounts and haven't yet calculated the possibility of getting pensions and Social Securities, this would just be cherry on top.

These are just some ideas on how to design a strategy. Your strategy could be completely different based on your situation and personal financial circumstances. The only rule of retirement is to never run out of money.

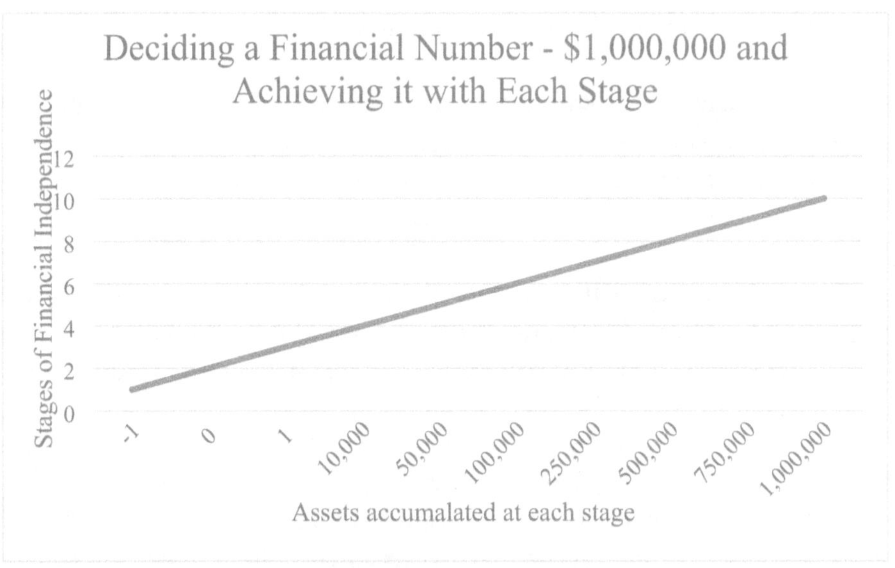

Early retirement is a long but achievable process. To get there, you can make a checklist for yourself and start crossing off what you achieve. There are stages, and these stages make it a process. Knowing all of the stages for yourself is important because when you start it can be quite overwhelming, your goal looks so far away and can be intimidating. However, breaking everything down into pieces to make it look more achievable will make things less daunting.

These stages will help you to continue moving towards your goal. First, let's see how you are going to calculate your magic saving number. You will estimate your yearlong expenses, and when you get that number, you will multiply it by 25. The answer will be your financial independence number. You will need to reach this number to be an early retiree. For example, your annual expenses are $40,000. Multiply this number by 25, and the answer is 1 million dollars. This is the amount of money you would need to have in the form of assets or investments to reach your goal. Early retirement means your portfolios are growing at an average rate of 7%, and you only take out 4% of it so this way it would keep growing. Once you have your magic number you can see what stage you are starting off at.

The first stage of early retirement is where most people start. This is when you have a negative net worth, which means your debt is more than your assets. You need to assemble your goals and access your standing point. For most people, this debt is student loans.

The next stage is having a net worth equal to zero. This means your assets and debts are equal. This goes for people who live paycheck to paycheck too. Studies show that most Americans are either at this stage or below zero.

The third stage is where your net worth is positive by at least $1. This doesn't seem like a big deal, but as I said earlier, most Americans are stuck at nothing. When your net worth is positive, it means your assets are more than your debts, even by a single dollar. This single dollar can get you going and grow into one big money tree.

The next stage is where your net worth is $10,000. This is a crucial point because just that extra zero of 10,000 being a five-digit number is very psychologically stimulating. When you add your debts and assets and your assets are higher than your debts by $10K you are starting to make progress.

Stage five is when your net worth gets to $50,000. This is a number that a lot of people make in a year. Once you reach this stage it means you have saved enough money for at least one year of living expenses. Congratulations!

The sixth stage is when your net worth is 10% off your financial independence number. If someone's financial independence number is 1 million dollars, 10% of that would be $100,000. It means that if you lost your job, you would be able to live of your investment for 2.5 years. This is why it is vital to have a certain number and to break it down into stages. Reaching stage six will open up answers to even more options that you have at this stage. This stage gives you the freedom to make more choices like thinking about whether you want to take some time off or change your job.

Stage seven is when your net worth is 25% of your financial freedom number. It would be $250,000 if you have a million-dollar goal. This will allow you to live off of your investment for six years without any job and no other assets as well. 25% is a huge milestone because things tend to move more quickly from here. You will see that 25% will turn into 50% and 75% very fast.

In step eight, your net worth will reach 50% of your financial independence number. This is huge because you will have a tremendous amount of confidence when you get here. But you may also get overwhelmed. It is human nature to try and move things along quickly when the halfway point is reached. Don't do anything silly like taking on too many obligations or quitting your job too early, stay focused.

Stage nine is when you reach 75% of your financial independence number. This is a significant achievement. It means that if you never touch that money and don't invest more in the stock market, your amount will double over seven years from the power of compound interest. In other words, if you don't save anything else for early retirement, in seven years, you will reach your goal anyway. But it is so important that when you reach this stage, you will still be contributing.

The final stage of your journey is when your net worth and your assets are 100% of your financial number. This would be such a fantastic moment for you. You will be surprised at how fast you got there. You made it!

Conclusion

I have covered every aspect of early retirement in the above chapters. The main thing that is imperative in this journey is consistency. You must stay away from the culture of consumerism. People may say that what you are doing is silly, but for your goal, you have to stay focused. Then obviously, you will need to pay yourself first. This must be done at the very beginning every time you make your budget. Next, you must start saving. Begin saving 15% to 20%, but over time you should increase this to as much as you can. For contributing to your savings, you must cut down your expenses, make more money, and of course save more money. To cut your costs, look at your budget and see the small places that you can work on. But don't forget to work with your significant expenses like transportation, traveling, food, and housing too. There is always room for some savings. Take all of your savings and invest it as much as you can. I am not talking about regular savings accounts. I have told you about investment accounts, how they differ and which ones to focus on. Investing in the stock market is key. Find ways to earn more. This can be done with side hustles and passive income. Side hustles are usually enjoyable and can even be done after retiring. Credit card hacking and travel hacking will save you a significant amount of money too. Lastly, have a retirement plan to help you live off your investments in a stress-free way. Now that you know what to do, how quickly can you get free?

Author's Note

Early retirement is a journey that doesn't attract or appeal to many people. People usually have the idea of it being impossible for them. This is what I always thought too. When the idea first formed in the back of my mind, I knew that it wouldn't be easy for me to pin down everything related to a successful early retirement. But at the same time, I thought that there had to be a way for almost everyone to retire early if they knew how to do it in the right way. That was the point that solidified this half-formed idea into a book.

I have made sure to not create a book that is complicated with investing terms and strategies. I want everyone to understand the steps and feel like they could do it on their own. I was addicted to the idea of early retirement after its discovery. Through my own extensive personal research, I have gathered so much information that I knew I had to find a way to present it in a clear and quick way. If you feel that the people around you could do so much better in their financial lives just by having this book, then don't hesitate to share it with them.

Lastly, I want to say that everyone can retire early as long as they are committed, determined, and focused on your goal. This book can benefit you so much if you are willing and serious about working for your dream.